P9-DND-921

Life Lessons

from THE INSPIRED WORD of GOD

BOOK of
EPHESIANS

MAX LUCADO

General Editor

LIFE LESSONS FROM THE INSPIRED WORD OF GOD—BOOK OF EPHESIANS
Copyright © 1998, Word Publishing. All rights reserved. No portion of this book may be reproduced, stored in a retrieval system, or transmitted in any form or by any means—electronic, mechanical, photocopy, recording, or any other—except for brief quotations in printed reviews, without the prior permission of the publisher.

Scripture passages taken from:

The Holy Bible, *New Century Version* (NCV)
Copyright ©1987, 1988, 1991 by Word Publishing. All rights reserved.

The Holy Bible, *New King James Version* (NKJV)
Copyright © 1979, 1980, 1982 by Thomas Nelson. All rights reserved.

All excerpts used by permission.

Design and cover art—by Koechel Peterson and Associates, Inc., Minneapolis, Minnesota.

Produced with the assistance of the Livingstone Corporation.

ISBN: 0-8499-5326-X
Published by Word Publishing

All rights reserved. *Printed in the United States of America.*

TABLE OF CONTENTS

HOW TO STUDY THE BIBLE

BY MAX LUCADO

*T*his is a peculiar book you are hold-ing. Words crafted in another lan-guage. Deeds done in a distant era. Events recorded in a far-off land. Counsel offered to a foreign people. This is a peculiar book.

It's surprising that anyone reads it. It's too old. Some of its writings date back five thousand years. It's too bizarre. The book speaks of incredible floods, fires, earth-quakes, and people with supernatural abilities. It's too radical. The Bible calls for undying devotion to a carpenter who called himself God's Son.

Logic says this book shouldn't survive. Too old, too bizarre, too radical.

The Bible has been banned, burned, scoffed, and ridiculed. Scholars have mocked it as foolish. Kings have branded it as illegal. A thousand times over it the grave has been dug and the dirge has begun, but somehow the Bible never stays in the grave. Not only has it survived, it has thrived. It is the single most popular book in all of his-tory. It has been the best-selling book in the world for years!

There is no way on earth to explain it. Which perhaps is the only explanation. The answer? The Bible's durability is not found on earth; it is found in heaven. For the millions who have tested its claims and claimed its promises, there is but one answer—the Bible is God's book and God's voice.

As you read it, you would be wise to give some thought to two questions. What is the purpose of the Bible? and How do I study the Bible? Time spent reflecting on these two issues will greatly enhance your Bible study.

What is the purpose of the Bible?

Let the Bible itself answer that question.

Since you were a child you have known the Holy Scriptures which are able to make you wise. And that wisdom leads to salvation through faith in Christ Jesus.

(2 Tim. 3:15)

The purpose of the Bible? Salvation. God's highest passion is to get his children home. His book, the Bible, describes his plan of salvation. The purpose of the Bible is to proclaim God's plan and passion to save his children.

That is the reason this book has endured through the centuries. It dares to tackle the toughest questions about life: Where do I go after I die? Is there a God? What do I do with my fears? The Bible offers answers to these crucial questions. It is the treasure map that leads us to God's highest treasure, eternal life.

But how do we use the Bible? Countless copies of Scripture sit unread on bookshelves and nightstands simply because people don't know how to read it. What can we do to make the Bible real in our lives?

The clearest answer is found in the words of Jesus.

"Ask," he promised, *"and God will give to you. Search, and you will find. Knock, and the door will open for you."*

(Matt. 7:7)

The first step in understanding the Bible is asking God to help us. We should read prayerfully. If anyone understands God's Word, it is because of God and not the reader.

But the Helper will teach you everything and will cause you to remember all that I told you. The Helper is the Holy Spirit whom the Father will send in my name.

(John 14:26)

Before reading the Bible, pray. Invite God to speak to you. Don't go to Scripture looking for your idea, go searching for his.

Not only should we read the Bible prayerfully, we should read it carefully. *Search and you will find* is the pledge. The Bible is not a newspaper to be skimmed but rather a mine to be quarried. *Search for it like silver, and hunt for it like hidden treasure. Then you will understand respect for the Lord, and you will find that you know God* (Prov. 2:4).

Any worthy find requires effort. The Bible is no exception. To understand the Bible you don't have to be brilliant, but you must be willing to roll up your sleeves and search.

Be a worker who is not ashamed and who uses the true teaching in the right way.

(2 Tim. 2:15)

Here's a practical point. Study the Bible a bit at a time. Hunger is not satisfied by eating twenty-one meals in one sitting once a week. The body needs a steady diet to remain strong. So does the soul. When God sent food to his people in the wilderness, he didn't provide loaves already made. Instead, he sent them manna in the shape of *thin flakes like frost . . . on the desert ground* (Exod. 16:14).

God gave manna in limited portions.

God sends spiritual food the same way. He opens the heavens with just enough nutrients for today's hunger. He provides, *a command here, a command there. A rule here, a rule there. A little lesson here, a little lesson there* (Isa. 28:10).

Don't be discouraged if your reading reaps a small harvest. Some days a lesser portion is all that is needed. What is important is to search every day for that day's message. A steady diet of God's Word over a lifetime builds a healthy soul and mind.

A little girl returned from her first day at school. Her mom asked, "Did you learn anything?" "Apparently not enough," the girl responded, "I have to go back tomorrow and the next day and the next. . . ."

Such is the case with learning. And such is the case with Bible study. Understanding comes little by little over a lifetime.

There is a third step in understanding the Bible. After the asking and seeking comes the knocking. After you ask and search, then knock.

Knock, and the door will open for you.
(Matt. 7:7)

To knock is to stand at God's door. To make yourself available. To climb the steps, cross the porch, stand at the doorway, and volunteer. Knocking goes beyond the realm of thinking and into the realm of acting.

To knock is to ask, What can I do? How can I obey? Where can I go?

It's one thing to know what to do. It's another to do it. But for those who do it, those who choose to obey, a special reward awaits them.

The truly happy are those who carefully study God's perfect law that makes people free, and they continue to study it. They do not forget what they heard, but they obey what God's teaching says. Those who do this will be made happy.
(James 1:25)

What a promise. Happiness comes to those who do what they read! It's the same with medicine. If you only read the label but ignore the pills, it won't help. It's the same with food. If you only read the recipe but never cook, you won't be fed. And it's the same with the Bible. If you only read the words but never obey, you'll never know the joy God has promised.

Ask. Search. Knock. Simple, isn't it? Why don't you give it a try? If you do, you'll see why you are holding the most remarkable book in history.

EPHESIANS

INTRODUCTION

I've just witnessed a beautiful wedding. The most beautiful I've ever seen. That says a lot, since I've seen a lot. Ministers see many weddings. It's a perk of the profession.

Is there anything more elegant than a wedding? Candles bathe a chapel in gold. Loving families fill the pews. Groomsmen and bridesmaids descend the aisles with bouquets of newness and rings of promise. What an occasion.

And nothing quite compares with that moment when the bride stands at the top of the aisle. Arm entwined with her father's, she takes those final steps with him and steps toward a new life with *her groom.*

Ahhh, the glory of a wedding. So to say I just saw the most beautiful one is no small thing. What made these nuptials so unforgettable? The groom. Usually the groom is not the star of the wedding. The fellow is typically upstaged by the girl. But this wedding was made special by the groom. It was enhanced by something he did.

And who he was made what he did even more startling. You see, he's a cowboy: a stocky fellow who went to college on a rodeo scholarship. But the one standing by me was not a macho calf roper, but a pinch-me-I'm-dreaming boy who'd never seen a bride so gorgeous.

He was composed as he walked down the aisle. He was fine as he took his place at the altar.

But when he saw the bride, he wept.

It was the moment he'd dreamed of. It was as if he'd been given life's greatest gift—a bride in all her beauty. By the way, those are the very words Paul uses to describe the church: a bride in all her beauty.

"He [Jesus] died so he could give the church to himself like a bride in all her beauty. He died so that the church could be pure and without fault, with no evil or sin or any other wrong thing in it" (Ephesians 5:27).

Ponder that verse. Jesus died for a bride. He died so he could be married. This passage anticipates the day when the groom will see his bride—when Christ will receive his church. Jesus' fondest longing will be fulfilled. His Bride will arrive.

The letter to the Ephesians celebrates the beauty of the church—the Bride of Christ. From our perspective the church isn't so pretty. We see the backbiting, the squabbling, the divisions. Heaven sees that, as well. But heaven sees more. Heaven sees the church as cleansed and made holy by Christ.

Heaven sees the church ascending to heaven. Heaven sees the Bride wearing the spotless gown of Jesus Christ.

It's enough to make one weep.

LESSON ONE

WHERE DO YOU BELONG?

REFLECTION

Begin your study by sharing thoughts on this question.

1. Think of a time when you felt a sense of belonging to a group of people. What does it feel like to belong?

_____

_____

_____

BIBLE READING

Read Ephesians 1:1–14 from the NCV or the NKJV.

NCV

¹From Paul, an apostle of Christ Jesus. I am an apostle because that is what God wanted.

To God's holy people living in Ephesus, believers in Christ Jesus:

²Grace and peace to you from God our Father and the Lord Jesus Christ.

³Praise be to the God and Father of our Lord Jesus Christ. In Christ, God has given us every spiritual blessing in the heavenly world. ⁴That is, in Christ, he chose us before the world was

NKJV

Paul, an apostle of Jesus Christ by the will of God,

To the saints who are in Ephesus, and faithful in Christ Jesus:

²Grace to you and peace from God our Father and the Lord Jesus Christ.

³Blessed *be* the God and Father of our Lord Jesus Christ, who has blessed us with every

NCV

made so that we would be his holy people—people without blame before him. [5]Because of his love, God had already decided to make us his own children through Jesus Christ. That was what he wanted and what pleased him, [6]and it brings praise to God because of his wonderful grace. God gave that grace to us freely, in Christ, the One he loves. [7]In Christ we are set free by the blood of his death, and so we have forgiveness of sins. How rich is God's grace, [8]which he has given to us so fully and freely. God, with full wisdom and understanding, [9]let us know his secret purpose. This was what God wanted, and he planned to do it through Christ. [10]His goal was to carry out his plan, when the right time came, that all things in heaven and on earth would be joined together in Christ as the head.

[11]In Christ we were chosen to be God's people, because from the very beginning God had decided this in keeping with his plan. And he is the One who makes everything agree with what he decides and wants. [12]We are the first people who hoped in Christ, and we were chosen so that we would bring praise to God's glory. [13]So it is with you. When you heard the true teaching—the Good News about your salvation—you believed in Christ. And in Christ, God put his special mark of ownership on you by giving you the Holy Spirit that he had promised. [14]That Holy Spirit is the guarantee that we will receive what God promised for his people until God gives full freedom to those who are his—to bring praise to God's glory.

NKJV

spiritual blessing in the heavenly *places* in Christ, [4]just as He chose us in Him before the foundation of the world, that we should be holy and without blame before Him in love, [5]having predestined us to adoption as sons by Jesus Christ to Himself, according to the good pleasure of His will, [6]to the praise of the glory of His grace, by which He has made us accepted in the Beloved.

[7]In Him we have redemption through His blood, the forgiveness of sins, according to the riches of His grace [8]which He made to abound toward us in all wisdom and prudence, [9]having made known to us the mystery of His will, according to His good pleasure which He purposed in Himself, [10]that in the dispensation of the fullness of the times He might gather together in one all things in Christ, both which are in heaven and which are on earth—in Him. [11]In Him also we have obtained an inheritance, being predestined according to the purpose of Him who works all things according to the counsel of His will, [12]that we who first trusted in Christ should be to the praise of His glory.

[13]In Him you also *trusted,* after you heard the word of truth, the gospel of your salvation; in whom also, having believed, you were sealed with the Holy Spirit of promise, [14]who is the guarantee of our inheritance until the redemption of the purchased possession, to the praise of His glory.

DISCOVERY

Explore the Bible reading by discussing these questions.

2. What are some spiritual blessings that we have through Christ?

    _____

    _____

    _____

3. God forgives our sins through the blood of Christ. What difference does that make in our daily life?

    _____

    _____

    _____

4. What is special about the fact that God deliberately *chooses* us as his people?

    _____

    _____

    _____

5. How does God choose his people?

    _____

    _____

    _____

6. In what way is the Holy Spirit God's mark of ownership on us?

_____

_____

_____

INSPIRATION

Here's an uplifting thought from *The Inspirational Bible*.

We all desire relationships in which we are accepted, valued, and wanted. We desperately long for this esteem from our peers, but seldom experience the "real thing."

Countless stories are written about teenagers who accept life-threatening dares in the hopes of being accepted by their peers, or business people who compromise their integrity and ethics to join an elite, inner circle. We read of men and women who are driven to succeed because they believe the lie that says their value is determined by the quality and level of their performance. Or how about the teenager or lonely single who sacrifices his virginity for the chance to experience closeness and the feeling of being wanted?

For the Christian, none of this futile struggle is necessary because we have been chosen by God before time ever began. We belong, we matter, we have been accepted. No longer outcasts or second-class citizens, we are part of his family.

(From *A Dad's Blessing*
by Gary Smalley and John Trent)

RESPONSE

Use these questions to share more deeply with each other.

7. Describe being unwanted.

_____

_____

_____

8. Describe being valued.

_____

_____

_____

9. Why does God value us?

_____

_____

_____

PRAYER

Thank you, God, for choosing us. May we be spurred on by your love to do great works, yet never substitute those works for your great grace. May we always hear your voice. Keep us amazed and mesmerized by what you have done for us.

JOURNALING

Take a few moments to record your personal insights from this lesson.

What situations will I face more effectively this week if I remember that I am chosen and valued by God?

ADDITIONAL QUESTIONS

10. What conclusions can you draw from the statement that God chose us before the foundation of the world?

_____

_____

_____

11. In what ways do we bring praise to God's glory?

_____

_____

_____

12. Describe someone who has exemplified God's grace to you.

_____

_____

_____

For more Bible passages on being God's child, see John 1:11–13; Romans 8:15–17; Galatians 3:26–4:7; Hebrews 12:8–11.

To complete the Book of Ephesians during this twelve-part study, read Ephesians 1:1–14.

ADDITIONAL THOUGHTS

LESSON TWO

THE POWER OF OUR FAITH

REFLECTION

Begin your study by sharing thoughts on this question.

1. Think of someone who has a powerful faith. What are the evidences of his or her faith?

_____

_____

_____

BIBLE READING

Read Ephesians 1:15–23 from the NCV or the NKJV.

NCV	NKJV
¹⁵That is why since I heard about your faith in the Lord Jesus and your love for all God's people, ¹⁶I have not stopped giving thanks to God for you. I always remember you in my prayers, ¹⁷asking the God of our Lord Jesus Christ, the glorious Father, to give you a spirit of wisdom and revelation so that you will know him better. ¹⁸I pray also that you will have greater understanding in your heart so you will know the hope to which he has called us and	¹⁵Therefore I also, after I heard of your faith in the Lord Jesus and your love for all the saints, ¹⁶do not cease to give thanks for you, making mention of you in my prayers:¹⁷that the God of our Lord Jesus Christ, the Father of glory, may give to you the spirit of wisdom and revelation in the knowledge of Him, ¹⁸the eyes of your understanding being enlightened; that you may know what is the hope of His calling, what are the riches of the glory of His inheritance in

NCV

that you will know how rich and glorious are the blessings God has promised his holy people. [19]And you will know that God's power is very great for us who believe. That power is the same as the great strength [20]God used to raise Christ from the dead and put him at his right side in the heavenly world. [21]God has put Christ over all rulers, authorities, powers, and kings, not only in this world but also in the next. [22]God put everything under his power and made him the head over everything for the church, [23]which is Christ's body. The church is filled with Christ, and Christ fills everything in every way.

NKJV

the saints, [19]and what *is* the exceeding greatness of His power toward us who believe, according to the working of His mighty power [20]which He worked in Christ when He raised Him from the dead and seated *Him* at His right hand in the heavenly *places,* [21]far above all principality and power and might and dominion, and every name that is named, not only in this age but also in that which is to come.

[22]And He put all *things* under His feet, and gave Him *to be* head over all *things* to the church, [23]which is His body, the fullness of Him who fills all in all.

DISCOVERY

Explore the Bible reading by discussing these questions.

2. Why does having faith make a difference in our lives?

_____

_____

_____

3. Paul prayed for the Ephesians to have a spirit of wisdom and revelation to know God better. Describe the process of knowing God better.

_____

_____

_____

4. What rich and glorious blessings promised by God do you hold onto in your life?

_____

_____

_____

5. The same power that raised Christ from the dead works through our faith. In what way should we be using the power of our faith?

_____

_____

_____

6. If God is over all rulers, kings, and powers in this world, why do evil dictators exist?

_____

_____

_____

INSPIRATION

Here is an uplifting thought from *The Inspirational Bible.*

The fact that God has chosen some to be saved does not mean that He has chosen the rest to be lost. The world is already lost and dead in sins. If left to ourselves, all of us would be condemned eternally. The question is, Does God have a right to stoop down, take a handful of already doomed clay, and fashion a vessel of beauty out of it? Of course He does. C. R. Erdman put it in right perspective when he said, "God's sovereignty is never exercised in condemning men who ought to be saved, but rather it has resulted in the salvation of men who ought to be lost."

The only way people can know if they are among the elect is by trusting Jesus Christ as Lord and Savior (1 Thessalonians 1:4–7). God holds people responsible to accept the Savior by an act of the will. In reproving those Jews who did not believe, Jesus placed the blame on their will. He did *not* say, "You cannot come to Me because you are not chosen." Rather, He *did* say, "You *are not willing* to come to Me that you may have life" (John 5:40, emphasis added).

The real question of a believer is not, Does the sovereign God have the right to choose people to be saved? Rather, it is, Why did He choose *me*? This should make a person a worshiper for all eternity.

(From *Alone in Majesty* by William MacDonald)

RESPONSE

Use these questions to share more deeply with each other.

7. How does God's sovereignty and man's will co-exist?

_____

_____

_____

8. In what sense is our salvation an act of our will?

_____

_____

_____

9. What about your salvation causes you to worship God?

_____

_____

_____

PRAYER

Blessed Lord and God, we come to you, aware that you rule our world. You became flesh, dwelled among us, saw us in our fallen state, and reached in and pulled us out. You offered us salvation; you offered us mercy. And we are ever thankful.

JOURNALING

Take a few moments to record your personal insights from this lesson.

In what ways am I thankful for my salvation?

ADDITIONAL QUESTIONS

10. Describe God's relationship to his church.

_____

_____

_____

11. How would Paul describe the faith you see around you today?

_____

_____

_____

12. In what way is the church filled with Christ?

_____

_____

_____

For more Bible passages on God's powerful salvation, see Romans 8:28–30; 1 Timothy 2:3–6; Titus 3:4–7.

To complete the Book of Ephesians during this twelve-part study, read Ephesians 1:15–23.

ADDITIONAL THOUGHTS

LESSON THREE

HAVE MERCY!

REFLECTION

Begin your study by sharing thoughts on this question.

1. Think of someone who is merciful. What typifies his or her life?

_____

_____

_____

BIBLE READING

Read Ephesians 2:1–10 from the NCV or the NKJV.

NCV

¹In the past you were spiritually dead because of your sins and the things you did against God. ²Yes, in the past you lived the way the world lives, following the ruler of the evil powers that are above the earth. That same spirit is now working in those who refuse to obey God. ³In the past all of us lived like them, trying to please our sinful selves and doing all the things our bodies and minds wanted. We should have suffered God's anger because of the way we were. We were the same as all other people.

NKJV

¹And you *He made alive,* who were dead in trespasses and sins, ²in which you once walked according to the course of this world, according to the prince of the power of the air, the spirit who now works in the sons of disobedience, ³among whom also we all once conducted ourselves in the lusts of our flesh, fulfilling the desires of the flesh and of the mind, and were by nature children of wrath, just as the others.

⁴But God, who is rich in mercy, because of His great love with which He loved us, ⁵even

NCV

⁴But God's mercy is great, and he loved us very much. ⁵Though we were spiritually dead because of the things we did against God, he gave us new life with Christ. You have been saved by God's grace. ⁶And he raised us up with Christ and gave us a seat with him in the heavens. He did this for those in Christ Jesus ⁷so that for all future time he could show the very great riches of his grace by being kind to us in Christ Jesus. ⁸I mean that you have been saved by grace through believing. You did not save yourselves; it was a gift from God. ⁹It was not the result of your own efforts, so you cannot brag about it. ¹⁰God has made us what we are. In Christ Jesus, God made us to do good works, which God planned in advance for us to live our lives doing.

NKJV

when we were dead in trespasses, made us alive together with Christ (by grace you have been saved), ⁶and raised *us* up together, and made *us* sit together in the heavenly *places* in Christ Jesus, ⁷that in the ages to come He might show the exceeding riches of His grace in *His* kindness toward us in Christ Jesus. ⁸For by grace you have been saved through faith, and that not of yourselves; *it is* the gift of God, ⁹not of works, lest anyone should boast. ¹⁰For we are His workmanship, created in Christ Jesus for good works, which God prepared beforehand that we should walk in them.

DISCOVERY

Explore the Bible reading by discussing these questions.

2. What is something you did in the past but would never do now specifically because you are a Christian?

_____

_____

_____

3. Why does sin anger God?

_____

_____

_____

4. In what sense is "spiritually dead" an accurate description of life without faith in Christ?

_____

_____

_____

5. Salvation is described here as a gift, a kindness from God. In what way is our salvation like a present?

_____

_____

_____

6. Why do we sometimes perceive our salvation to be related to our own efforts?

_____

_____

_____

INSPIRATION

Here is an uplifting thought from *The Inspirational Bible*.

When I read a verse like Ephesians 2:4, I feel I have discovered God's roadblock on one's way to hell—[But God's mercy is great.] He is so rich in mercy that none need perish, but individuals must come to God in his appointed way. I adore the mercy that had lovingkindness, pity and compassion on me. And I praise Him for the mercies of life—for sight, hearing, smell, memory, appetite, soundness of body and mind, food, drink, and all the wonders of nature.

As always, privilege brings responsibility. God wants us to imitate Him in this quality of mercy. He wants us to be merciful to one another. "Therefore be merciful, just as your Father also is merciful" (Luke 6:36).

Let me give you a modern illustration of mercy in action. One day, a Christian named Paul went into a coffee shop, sat on a stool, and ordered his lunch. When he began speaking to the man next to him, he realized that Fred was in deep spiritual need. After sharing the gospel with him, Paul arranged to meet him again. It was at the second meeting that Fred was converted. Then Paul began to disciple him on a one-on-one basis, and Fred grew in grace and in knowledge of the Lord Jesus. But it wasn't long before Fred learned that he had a life-threatening disease. He had to go to a convalescent hospital that was sadly substandard. Paul visited him regularly, bathed him, changed the sheets, and did other chores that the staff should have been doing. The night Fred died, Paul was holding him in his arms, whispering verses of Scripture in his ear. That's mercy. It's a wonderful thing to see that Godlike quality in a human life.

(From *Alone In Majesty*
by William MacDonald)

RESPONSE

Use these questions to share more deeply with each other.

7. Describe an act of mercy you have seen recently.

_____

_____

_____

8. Think of a time when you had the opportunity to show mercy but didn't. Why didn't you?

_____

_____

_____

9. If God were not merciful, what would our lives be like?

_____

_____

_____

PRAYER

Here we are, Father. We call ourselves your people, yet we carry the baggage of a week of concerns. We come to you just as we are, without trying to hide our mistakes and our weaknesses. We need your mercy and grace. Father, mend us and make us better than we could be alone.

JOURNALING

Take a few moments to record your personal insights from this lesson.

Where can I show more mercy through my life?

ADDITIONAL QUESTIONS

10. What is the danger of a faith based on works?

_____

_____

_____

11. What was your life like before you were saved?

_____

_____

_____

12. How can we as Christians show the great riches of God's grace?

_____

_____

_____

For more Bible passages on God's mercy, see Nehemiah 9:29–31; Micah 7:18–20; Luke 6:34–36; 1 Timothy 1:15–17; 1 Peter 3:9.

To complete the Book of Ephesians during this twelve-part study, read Ephesians 2:1–10.

ADDITIONAL THOUGHTS

LESSON FOUR

FAMILY TIES AND RACIAL BLURS

REFLECTION

Begin your study by sharing thoughts on this idea.

1. Describe some of your best family memories.

_____

_____

_____

BIBLE READING

Read Ephesians 2:11–22 from the NCV or the NKJV.

NCV

[11]You were not born Jewish. You are the people the Jews call "uncircumcised." Those who call you "uncircumcised" call themselves "circumcised." (Their circumcision is only something they themselves do on their bodies.) [12]Remember that in the past you were without Christ. You were not citizens of Israel, and you had no part in the agreements with the promise that God made to his people. You had no hope, and you did not know God. [13]But now in Christ Jesus, you who were far away from

NKJV

[11]Therefore remember that you, once Gentiles in the flesh—who are called Uncircumcision by what is called the Circumcision made in the flesh by hands—[12]that at that time you were without Christ, being aliens from the commonwealth of Israel and strangers from the covenants of promise, having no hope and without God in the world. [13]But now in Christ Jesus you who once were far off have been brought near by the blood of Christ.

[14]For He Himself is our peace, who has

NCV

God are brought near through the blood of Christ's death. ¹⁴Christ himself is our peace. He made both Jewish people and those who are not Jews one people. They were separated as if there were a wall between them, but Christ broke down that wall of hate by giving his own body. ¹⁵The Jewish law had many commands and rules, but Christ ended that law. His purpose was to make the two groups of people become one new people in him and in this way make peace. ¹⁶It was also Christ's purpose to end the hatred between the two groups, to make them into one body, and to bring them back to God. Christ did all this with his death on the cross. ¹⁷Christ came and preached peace to you who were far away from God, and to those who were near to God. ¹⁸Yes, it is through Christ we all have the right to come to the Father in one Spirit.

¹⁹Now you who are not Jewish are not foreigners or strangers any longer, but are citizens together with God's holy people. You belong to God's family. ²⁰You are like a building that was built on the foundation of the apostles and prophets. Christ Jesus himself is the most important stone in that building, ²¹and that whole building is joined together in Christ. He makes it grow and become a holy temple in the Lord. ²²And in Christ you, too, are being built together with the Jews into a place where God lives through the Spirit.

NKJV

made both one, and has broken down the middle wall of separation, ¹⁵having abolished in His flesh the enmity, *that is,* the law of commandments *contained* in ordinances, so as to create in Himself one new man *from* the two, *thus* making peace, ¹⁶and that He might reconcile them both to God in one body through the cross, thereby putting to death the enmity. ¹⁷And He came and preached peace to you who were afar off and to those who were near. ¹⁸For through Him we both have access by one Spirit to the Father.

¹⁹Now, therefore, you are no longer strangers and foreigners, but fellow citizens with the saints and members of the household of God, ²⁰having been built on the foundation of the apostles and prophets, Jesus Christ Himself being the chief corner*stone,* ²¹in whom the whole building, being joined together, grows into a holy temple in the Lord, ²²in whom you also are being built together for a dwelling place of God in the Spirit.

DISCOVERY

Explore the Bible reading by discussing these questions.

2. List some distinctives of Jews and Gentiles.

_____

_____

_____

3. In what ways is Christ our "peace"?

_____

_____

_____

4. Before Christ's death the Jewish nation judged their righteousness by their obedience to numerous laws, regulations, and sacrifices. In what way did Christ's life and death change that concept of righteousness?

_____

_____

_____

5. Christ's death and resurrection changed the way we approach God from creatures to children. Describe the difference.

_____

_____

_____

6. This passage describes the church of Christ as a building of many stones. How does that analogy work well in describing the church today?

_____

_____

_____

INSPIRATION

Here is an uplifting thought from *The Inspirational Bible.*

We specialize in "I am right" rallies. We write books about what the other does wrong. We major in finding gossip and become experts in unveiling weaknesses. We split into little huddles and then, God forbid, we split again....

Are our differences that divisive? Are our opinions that obtrusive? Are our walls that wide? Is it *that* impossible to find a common cause?

"May they all be one," Jesus prayed.

One. Not one in groups of two thousand. But one in One. *One* church. *One* faith. *One* Lord.

Not Baptist, not Methodist, not Adventist. Just Christian. No denominations. No hierarchies. No traditions. Just Christ.

Too idealistic? Impossible to achieve? I don't think so. Harder things have been done, you know. For example, once upon a tree, a Creator gave his life for his creation. Maybe all we need are a few hearts that are willing to follow suit.

(From *No Wonder They Call Him the Savior* by Max Lucado)

RESPONSE

Use these questions to share more deeply with each other.

7. What were the racial implications of the peace Christ brought?

_____

_____

_____

8. One of the efforts of Christ was to end hatred. In what ways can the church today help that effort?

_____

_____

_____

9. List the best benefits to you of belonging to God's family.

_____

_____

_____

PRAYER

Father, as we set about the task of being your people, we pray that you'll help us. May we glorify your name. May we be open-minded. May we be sincere. May we be willing to change and grow. We thank you, Lord, for the privilege of being your family.

JOURNALING

Take a few moments to record your personal insights from this lesson.

What are my privileges and responsibilities in belonging to God's family?

ADDITIONAL QUESTIONS

10. How could a non-Jew have been saved before Christ's death?

_____

_____

_____

11. In what way is Jesus the cornerstone of the church?

_____

_____

_____

12. How did Christ's death give us the right to come to God as our father?

_____

_____

_____

For more Bible passages on God's family, see Acts 13:44–48; Romans 8:13–17; 2 Corinthians 5:14–15; Galatians 3:26–29; 1 Timothy 2:3–4.

To complete the Book of Ephesians during this twelve-part study, read Ephesians 2:11–22.

ADDITIONAL THOUGHTS

LESSON FIVE

GOD HAD A SECRET?

REFLECTION

Begin your study by sharing thoughts on this question.

1. Think of a time when someone gave you a surprise party or gift he had worked on in secret. How did you feel when you received it?

_____

_____

_____

BIBLE READING

Read Ephesians 3:1–13 from the NCV or the NKJV.

NCV

¹So I, Paul, am a prisoner of Christ Jesus for you who are not Jews. ²Surely you have heard that God gave me this work through his grace to help you. ³He let me know his secret by showing it to me. I have already written a little about this. ⁴If you read what I wrote then, you can see that I truly understand the secret about the Christ. ⁵People who lived in other times were not told that secret. But now, through the Spirit, God has shown that secret to his holy apostles and prophets. ⁶This is that secret: that

NKJV

¹For this reason I, Paul, the prisoner of Christ Jesus for you Gentiles—²if indeed you have heard of the dispensation of the grace of God which was given to me for you, ³how that by revelation He made known to me the mystery (as I have briefly written already, ⁴by which, when you read, you may understand my knowledge in the mystery of Christ), ⁵which in other ages was not made known to the sons of men, as it has now been revealed by the Spirit to His holy apostles and prophets: ⁶that the

NCV

through the Good News those who are not Jews will share with the Jews in God's blessing. They belong to the same body, and they share together in the promise that God made in Christ Jesus.

[7]By God's special gift of grace given to me through his power, I became a servant to tell that Good News. [8]I am the least important of all God's people, but God gave me this gift— to tell those who are not Jews the Good News about the riches of Christ, which are too great to understand fully. [9]And God gave me the work of telling all people about the plan for his secret, which has been hidden in him since the beginning of time. He is the One who created everything. [10]His purpose was that through the church all the rulers and powers in the heavenly world will now know God's wisdom, which has so many forms. [11]This agrees with the purpose God had since the beginning of time, and he carried out his plan through Christ Jesus our Lord. [12]In Christ we can come before God with freedom and without fear. We can do this through faith in Christ. [13]So I ask you not to become discouraged because of the sufferings I am having for you. My sufferings are for your glory.

NKJV

Gentiles should be fellow heirs, of the same body, and partakers of His promise in Christ through the gospel, [7]of which I became a minister according to the gift of the grace of God given to me by the effective working of His power.

[8]To me, who am less than the least of all the saints, this grace was given, that I should preach among the Gentiles the unsearchable riches of Christ, [9]and to make all see what *is* the fellowship of the mystery, which from the beginning of the ages has been hidden in God who created all things through Jesus Christ; [10]to the intent that now the manifold wisdom of God might be made known by the church to the principalities and powers in the heavenly *places,* [11]according to the eternal purpose which He accomplished in Christ Jesus our Lord, [12]in whom we have boldness and access with confidence through faith in Him. [13]Therefore I ask that you do not lose heart at my tribulations for you, which is your glory.

DISCOVERY

Explore the Bible reading by discussing these questions.

2. Paul, a Jew, became a missionary to the Gentiles at a time when the Jewish people found their identity in the fact that they were God's only chosen people. What consequences might Paul have had to pay for his actions?

_____

_____

_____

3. Why did Paul describe God's plan (to offer all people salvation) a "secret"?

_____

_____

_____

4. Why might the Jewish leaders have felt threatened by Paul's insistence that God included all people in his promise of salvation?

_____

_____

_____

5. Give your ideas about why Paul said he was the least important of all God's people.

_____

_____

_____

6. Through Christ, man can come to God in freedom and without fear. In what ways is that different from coming to God before Christ's incarnation?

_____

_____

_____

INSPIRATION

Here is an uplifting thought from *The Inspirational Bible*.

The promises of God's love and forgiveness are as real, as sure, as positive as human words can make them. But like describing the ocean, its total beauty cannot be understood until it is actually seen. It is the same with God's love. Until you actually accept it, until you actually experience it, until you actually possess true peace with God, no one can describe its wonders to you.

It is not something that you can do with your mind. Your finite mind is not capable of dealing with anything as great as the love of God. Your mind might have difficulty explaining how a black cow can eat green grass and give white milk—but you drink the milk and are nourished by it. Your mind can't reason through all the intricate processes that take place when you plant a small flat seed and it produces a huge vine, bearing luscious red and green watermelons—but you eat them and enjoy them! You can't understand radio, but you listen. Your mind can't explain the electricity that may be creating the light by which you are reading at this very moment—but you know that it's there and that it is making it possible for you to read!

(From *Peace with God*
by Billy Graham)

RESPONSE

Use these questions to share more deeply with each other.

7. The secret of God's salvation is really too great for us to understand. On what, then, is our faith in God's salvation and love based?

_____

_____

_____

8. What are some examples in your everyday world of things that you use or benefit from, even though you do not understand them?

_____

_____

_____

9. In what ways would you describe God's love to someone who has never heard of God?

_____

_____

_____

PRAYER

Father, we look at your plan and see that it's all based on your love, not on our performance. Help us understand that. Teach us to be captivated by your love. Allow us to be overwhelmed by your grace. Remind us to live grateful lives. Amen.

JOURNALING

Take a few moments to record your personal insights from this lesson.

In what situations or times in my life have I felt the most loved by God?

ADDITIONAL QUESTIONS

10. What kind of suffering was Paul referring to in the last verse of this passage?

_____

_____

_____

11. In what ways is God's salvation through Christ not a secret at all?

_____

_____

_____

12. How does God's wisdom appear in different forms?

_____

_____

_____

For more Bible passages on God's provision through Christ, see Psalm 6:4; John 3:16; 15:12; Romans 5:8; 8:35–37; 1 John 3:1.

To complete the Book of Ephesians during this twelve-part study, read Ephesians 3:1–13.

ADDITIONAL THOUGHTS

LESSON SIX

THE AMAZING LOVE OF CHRIST

REFLECTION

Begin your study by sharing thoughts on this question.

1. Describe the last time someone's love amazed you.

_____

_____

_____

BIBLE READING

Read Ephesians 3:14–21 from the NCV or the NKJV.

NCV

[14]So I bow in prayer before the Father [15]from whom every family in heaven and on earth gets its true name. [16]I ask the Father in his great glory to give you the power to be strong inwardly through his Spirit. [17]I pray that Christ will live in your hearts by faith and that your life will be strong in love and be built on love. [18]And I pray that you and all God's holy people will have the power to understand the greatness of Christ's love—how wide and how long and how high and how deep that love is.

NKJV

[14]For this reason I bow my knees to the Father of our Lord Jesus Christ, [15]from whom the whole family in heaven and earth is named, [16]that He would grant you, according to the riches of His glory, to be strengthened with might through His Spirit in the inner man, [17]that Christ may dwell in your hearts through faith; that you, being rooted and grounded in love, [18]may be able to comprehend with all the saints what *is* the width and length and depth and height—[19]to know the love of Christ which

NCV

[19]Christ's love is greater than anyone can ever know, but I pray that you will be able to know that love. Then you can be filled with the fullness of God.

[20]With God's power working in us, God can do much, much more than anything we can ask or imagine. [21]To him be glory in the church and in Christ Jesus for all time, forever and ever. Amen.

NKJV

passes knowledge; that you may be filled with all the fullness of God.

[20]Now to Him who is able to do exceedingly abundantly above all that we ask or think, according to the power that works in us, [21]to Him *be* glory in the church by Christ Jesus to all generations, forever and ever. Amen.

DISCOVERY

Explore the Bible reading by discussing these questions.

2. In what way does every family on heaven and earth get their true name from God?

_____

_____

_____

3. Paul prayed that the Ephesians would be strong inwardly through Christ's Spirit. Describe a person who fits that description.

_____

_____

_____

4. What are the hallmarks of our families and churches when we each build our lives on love, as Paul prayed?

_____

_____

_____

5. In what ways can we know Christ's love, even though we don't understand it?

_____

_____

_____

6. How can we be sure God's power is working through us rather than our own strength?

_____

_____

_____

INSPIRATION

Here's an uplifting thought from *The Inspirational Bible.*

Jesus was a master at communicating love and personal acceptance. He did so when He blessed and held . . . little children. But another time His sensitivity to touch someone was even more graphic. This was when Jesus met a grown man's need for meaningful touch, a man who was barred by law from ever touching anyone again. . . .

To touch a leper was unthinkable. Banishing lepers from society, people would not get within a stone's throw of them. (In fact, they would throw stones at them if they did come close!) . . . With their open sores and dirty bandages, lepers were the last persons anyone would want to touch. Yet the first thing Christ did for this man was touch him.

Even before Jesus spoke to him, He reached out His hand and touched him. Can you imagine what that scene must have looked like? Think how this man must have longed for someone to touch him, not throw stones at him to drive him away. Jesus could have healed him first and then touched him. But recognizing his deepest need, Jesus stretched out His hand even before He spoke words of physical and spiritual healing.

(From *The Gift of the Blessing* by Gary Smalley and John Trent)

RESPONSE

Use these questions to share more deeply with each other.

7.   Describe a time when you felt "touched" by the love of Christ.

_____

_____

_____

8. List some ways Christ showed his compassion during his earthly ministry.

_____

_____

_____

9. How can we live our lives so that we are most likely to experience the love of Christ?

_____

_____

_____

PRAYER

We're not perfect, Father, but we are yours. We claim your salvation and your grace. We ask you to make us every day into the image of Jesus Christ. Help us to walk this earth in love as he did. We are amazed at such mercy that forgives us time and time again. Thank you.

JOURNALING

Take a few moments to record your personal insights from this lesson.

How can I be more like Christ in the way I show love to the people around me?

ADDITIONAL QUESTIONS

10. To what do you compare the magnitude of Christ's love?

_____

_____

_____

11. How can we build our lives on love?

_____

_____

_____

12. List some ministries in the church today that reflect the way Jesus cared for the people around him.

_____

_____

_____

For more Bible passages on Christ's love, see Matthew 8:14–16; 9:35–38; 14:13–14; 17:6–8; 20:29–34; 23:37; Mark 10:13–16; Luke 7:12–13; 22:49–51; John 11:33–35.

To complete the Book of Ephesians during this twelve-part study, read Ephesians 3:14–21.

ADDITIONAL THOUGHTS

LESSON SEVEN

BODY PARTS EVERYWHERE

REFLECTION

Begin your study by sharing thoughts on this question.

1. Think about the people who serve your church through their natural gifts and
   abilities. What are some of the gifts they use for ministry?

_____

_____

_____

BIBLE READING

Read Ephesians 4:1–16 from the NCV or the NKJV.

NCV

¹I am in prison because I belong to the Lord.
God chose you to be his people, so I urge you
now to live the life to which God called you.
²Always be humble, gentle, and patient, accept-
ing each other in love. ³You are joined together
with peace through the Spirit, so make every
effort to continue together in this way. ⁴There
is one body and one Spirit, and God called you
to have one hope. ⁵There is one Lord, one faith,

NKJV

¹I, therefore, the prisoner of the Lord,
beseech you to walk worthy of the calling with
which you were called, ²with all lowliness and
gentleness, with longsuffering, bearing with
one another in love, ³endeavoring to keep the
unity of the Spirit in the bond of peace. ⁴*There
is* one body and one Spirit, just as you were
called in one hope of your calling; ⁵one Lord,
one faith, one baptism; ⁶one God and Father of

and one baptism. [6]There is one God and Father of everything. He rules everything and is everywhere and is in everything.

[7]Christ gave each one of us the special gift of grace, showing how generous he is. [8]That is why it says in the Scriptures,

"When he went up to the heights,
he led a parade of captives,
and he gave gifts to people."

[9]When it says, "He went up," what does it mean? It means that he first came down to the earth. [10]So Jesus came down, and he is the same One who went up above all the sky. Christ did that to fill everything with his presence. [11]And Christ gave gifts to people—he made some to be apostles, some to be prophets, some to go and tell the Good News, and some to have the work of caring for and teaching God's people. [12]Christ gave those gifts to prepare God's holy people for the work of serving, to make the body of Christ stronger. [13]This work must continue until we are all joined together in the same faith and in the same knowledge of the Son of God. We must become like a mature person, growing until we become like Christ and have his perfection.

[14]Then we will no longer be babies. We will not be tossed about like a ship that the waves carry one way and then another. We will not be influenced by every new teaching we hear from people who are trying to fool us. They make plans and try any kind of trick to fool people into following the wrong path. [15]No! Speaking the truth with love, we will grow up in every way into Christ, who is the head. [16]The whole body depends on Christ, and all the parts of the

all, who *is* above all, and through all, and in you all.

[7]But to each one of us grace was given according to the measure of Christ's gift. [8]Therefore He says:

"When He ascended on high,
He led captivity captive,
And gave gifts to men."

[9](Now this, "He ascended"—what does it mean but that He also first descended into the lower parts of the earth? [10]He who descended is also the One who ascended far above all the heavens, that He might fill all things.)

[11]And He Himself gave some *to be* apostles, some prophets, some evangelists, and some pastors and teachers, [12]for the equipping of the saints for the work of ministry, for the edifying of the body of Christ, [13]till we all come to the unity of the faith and of the knowledge of the Son of God, to a perfect man, to the measure of the stature of the fullness of Christ; [14]that we should no longer be children, tossed to and fro and carried about with every wind of doctrine, by the trickery of men, in the cunning craftiness of deceitful plotting, [15]but, speaking the truth in love, may grow up in all things into Him who is the head—Christ— [16]from whom the whole body, joined and knit together by what every joint supplies, according to the effective working by which every part does its share, causes growth of the body for the edifying of itself in love.

NCV

body are joined and held together. Each part does its own work to make the whole body grow and be strong with love.

NKJV

DISCOVERY

Explore the Bible reading by discussing these questions.

2. In what ways would you describe the life God calls us to live?

_____

_____

_____

3. List some ways we can accept each other in love.

_____

_____

_____

4. This passage tells us that we each have a special gift of grace. Can you identify your own gift of grace?

_____

_____

_____

5. The purpose of our gifts is to grow to maturity in Christ. In what ways do the gifts we have identified help us do that?

_____

_____

_____

6. If the church is like a body, this passage compares Christ to the head of the body. What part of the body are you?

_____

_____

_____

INSPIRATION

Here is an uplifting thought from *The Inspirational Bible*.

Most believers are convinced that it is the pastor's responsibility to bring people into the church as well as into the kingdom of God. Nothing could be further from the truth. The Scripture is clear on this point. Pastors were given by God to the church to equip the people to do the work. . . . Sermons are not God's primary method for reaching people. People are His method for reaching people. What kind of people? Men and women whose lives and life-styles have been deeply affected by the truths of Scripture, people who have discovered the wonderful Spirit-filled life.

God is looking for imperfect men and women who have learned to walk in moment-by-moment dependence on the Holy Spirit. Christians who have come to terms with their inadequacies, fears, and failures. Believers who have become discontent with "surviving" and have taken the time to investigate everything God has to offer in this life.

God's method for reaching this generation, and every generation, is not preachers and sermons. It is Christians whose life-styles are empowered and directed by the Holy Spirit. People are the key to reaching people!

(From *The Wonderful Spirit-Filled Life* by Charles Stanley)

RESPONSE

Use these questions to share more deeply with each other.

7. How do church staff members equip us to do God's work?

_____

_____

_____

8. Describe the Spirit-filled life.

_____

_____

_____

9. In what ways should we be using our gifts to reach others for Christ?

_____

_____

_____

PRAYER

Father, how holy and great is your promise. You've been so good to us and have gifted us richly. Renew our vision; help us to see heaven. Help us to be busy about the right business: the business of serving you.

JOURNALING

Take a few moments to record your personal insights from this lesson.

How can I use my gifts this week for God's glory?

ADDITIONAL QUESTIONS

10. What does it mean to be a spiritual baby?

_____

_____

_____

11. How does Christ function with the church like the head on a body?

_____

_____

_____

12. What keeps us from humility, gentleness, and patience?

_____

_____

_____

For more Bible passages on the purpose of our gifts, see Romans 12:3–6;
1 Corinthians 12:12; 14:26; 1 Timothy 4:14; 2 Timothy 1:6.

To complete the Book of Ephesians during this twelve-part study, read
Ephesians 4:1–16.

ADDITIONAL THOUGHTS

LESSON EIGHT

A PICTURE'S WORTH HOW MANY WORDS?

REFLECTION

Begin your study by sharing thoughts on this question.

1. Think of a time when someone's careless words hurt you (or vice versa). What was the effect on both of you?

_____

_____

_____

BIBLE READING

Read Ephesians 4:17–32 from the NCV or the NKJV.

NCV

[17]In the Lord's name, I tell you this. Do not continue living like those who do not believe. Their thoughts are worth nothing. [18]They do not understand, and they know nothing, because they refuse to listen. So they cannot have the life that God gives. [19]They have lost all feeling of shame, and they use their lives for doing evil. They continually want to do all kinds of evil. [20]But what you learned in Christ was not like this. [21]I know that you heard about

NKJV

[17]This I say, therefore, and testify in the Lord, that you should no longer walk as the rest of the Gentiles walk, in the futility of their mind, [18]having their understanding darkened, being alienated from the life of God, because of the ignorance that is in them, because of the blindness of their heart; [19]who, being past feeling, have given themselves over to lewdness, to work all uncleanness with greediness.

[20]But you have not so learned Christ, [21]if

NCV

him, and you are in him, so you were taught the truth that is in Jesus. ²²You were taught to leave your old self—to stop living the evil way you lived before. That old self becomes worse, because people are fooled by the evil things they want to do. ²³But you were taught to be made new in your hearts, ²⁴to become a new person. That new person is made to be like God—made to be truly good and holy.

²⁵So you must stop telling lies. Tell each other the truth, because we all belong to each other in the same body. ²⁶When you are angry, do not sin, and be sure to stop being angry before the end of the day. ²⁷Do not give the devil a way to defeat you. ²⁸Those who are stealing must stop stealing and start working. They should earn an honest living for themselves. Then they will have something to share with those who are poor.

²⁹When you talk, do not say harmful things, but say what people need—words that will help others become stronger. Then what you say will do good to those who listen to you. ³⁰And do not make the Holy Spirit sad. The Spirit is God's proof that you belong to him. God gave you the Spirit to show that God will make you free when the final day comes. ³¹Do not be bitter or angry or mad. Never shout angrily or say things to hurt others. Never do anything evil. ³²Be kind and loving to each other, and forgive each other just as God forgave you in Christ.

NKJV

indeed you have heard Him and have been taught by Him, as the truth is in Jesus: ²²that you put off, concerning your former conduct, the old man which grows corrupt according to the deceitful lusts, ²³and be renewed in the spirit of your mind, ²⁴and that you put on the new man which was created according to God, in true righteousness and holiness.

²⁵Therefore, putting away lying, "Let each one *of you* speak truth with his neighbor," for we are members of one another. ²⁶"Be angry, and do not sin": do not let the sun go down on your wrath, ²⁷nor give place to the devil. ²⁸Let him who stole steal no longer, but rather let him labor, working with *his* hands what is good, that he may have something to give him who has need. ²⁹Let no corrupt word proceed out of your mouth, but what is good for necessary edification, that it may impart grace to the hearers. ³⁰And do not grieve the Holy Spirit of God, by whom you were sealed for the day of redemption. ³¹Let all bitterness, wrath, anger, clamor, and evil speaking be put away from you, with all malice. ³²And be kind to one another, tenderhearted, forgiving one another, even as God in Christ forgave you.

DISCOVERY

Explore the Bible reading by discussing these questions.

2. Describe some evidences in our culture of a loss of shame.

_____

_____

_____

3. Define the "old self."

_____

_____

_____

4. What is the difference between the "old self" and the "new self"?

_____

_____

_____

5. In what ways do we give the devil a way to defeat us?

_____

_____

_____

6. This passage says we are not to be unkind with our words. What are we to be or do with our words, then?

_____

_____

_____

INSPIRATION

Here is an uplifting thought from *The Inspirational Bible*.

Insensitivity makes a wound that heals slowly.

If someone hurts your feelings intentionally, you know how to react. You know the source of the pain. But if someone accidentally bruises your soul, it's difficult to know how to respond.

Someone at work criticizes the new boss who also happens to be your dear friend. "Oh, I'm sorry—I forgot the two of you were so close."

A joke is told at a party about overweight people. You're overweight. You hear the joke. You smile politely while your heart sinks.

What was intended to be a reprimand for a decision or action becomes a personal attack.

"You have a history of poor decisions, John."

Someone chooses to wash your dirty laundry in public. "Sue, is it true that you and Jim are separated?"

Insensitive comments. Thoughts that should have remained thoughts. Feelings which had no business being expressed. Opinions carelessly tossed like a grenade into a crowd.

And if you were to tell the one who threw these thoughtless darts about the pain they caused, his response would be "Oh, but I had no intention. . . . I didn't realize you were so sensitive!" or "I forgot you were here."

In a way, the words are comforting, until you stop to think about them (which is not recommended). For when you start to think about insensitive slurs, you realize they come from an infamous family whose father has breeded generations of pain. His name? Egotism. His children? Three sisters: Disregard, disrespect, and disappointment.

These three witches have combined to poison countless relationships and break innumerable hearts. Listed among their weapons are Satan's cruelest artillery: gossip, accusations, resentment, impatience, and on and on. . . .

God's Word has strong medicine for those who carelessly wag their tongues. The message is clear: He who dares to call himself God's ambassador is not afforded the luxury of idle words. Excuses such as "I didn't know you were here" or "I didn't realize this was so touchy" are shallow when they come from those who claim to be followers and imitators of the Great Physician. We have an added responsibility to guard our tongues.

(From *God Came Near*
by Max Lucado)

RESPONSE

Use these questions to share more deeply with each other.

7. Why do we say things to hurt others, even though God clearly tells us not to in this passage?

_____

_____

_____

8. Why does it feel good at times to put others down?

_____

_____

_____

9. How does God view our actions when we disregard or disrespect each other?

_____

_____

_____

PRAYER

Father, we invite your assistance and guidance and powerful indwelling. We do not have the strength in ourselves to be transformed into your likeness and not be conformed to this world. Teach us to speak with your voice and love with your love.

JOURNALING

Take a few moments to record your personal insights from this lesson.

How do I disregard or disrespect through my words?

ADDITIONAL QUESTIONS

10. Is there a way to rid our lives of bitterness and anger?

_____

_____

_____

11. What kinds of words do others need from us?

_____

_____

_____

12. How are we fooled by the evil things we want to do?

_____

_____

_____

For more Bible passages on speech that pleases God, see Proverbs 16:24; 25:11; Ecclesiastes 10:12; Isaiah 50:4; Ephesians 4:29; Colossians 4:6.

To complete the Book of Ephesians during this twelve-part study, read Ephesians 4:17–32.

LESSON NINE

CHOOSING TO WALK IN THE LIGHT

REFLECTION

Begin your study by sharing thoughts on this question.

1. Think of the wisest people you know. What are the evidences of their wisdom?

_____

_____

_____

BIBLE READING

Read Ephesians 5:1–20 from the NCV or the NKJV.

NCV

¹You are God's children whom he loves, so try to be like him. ²Live a life of love just as Christ loved us and gave himself for us as a sweet-smelling offering and sacrifice to God.

³But there must be no sexual sin among you, or any kind of evil or greed. Those things are not right for God's holy people. ⁴Also, there must be no evil talk among you, and you must not speak foolishly or tell evil jokes. These things are not right for you. Instead, you should be giving thanks to God. ⁵You can be sure of

NKJV

¹Therefore be imitators of God as dear children. ²And walk in love, as Christ also has loved us and given Himself for us, an offering and a sacrifice to God for a sweet-smelling aroma.

³But fornication and all uncleanness or covetousness, let it not even be named among you, as is fitting for saints;⁴neither filthiness, nor foolish talking, nor coarse jesting, which are not fitting, but rather giving of thanks. ⁵For this you know, that no fornicator, unclean person, nor covetous man, who is an idolater,

this: No one will have a place in the kingdom of Christ and of God who sins sexually, or does evil things, or is greedy. Anyone who is greedy is serving a false god.

⁶Do not let anyone fool you by telling you things that are not true, because these things will bring God's anger on those who do not obey him. ⁷So have nothing to do with them. ⁸In the past you were full of darkness, but now you are full of light in the Lord. So live like children who belong to the light. ⁹Light brings every kind of goodness, right living, and truth. ¹⁰Try to learn what pleases the Lord. ¹¹Have nothing to do with the things done in darkness, which are not worth anything. But show that they are wrong. ¹²It is shameful even to talk about what those people do in secret. ¹³But the light makes all things easy to see, ¹⁴and everything that is made easy to see can become light. This is why it is said:

"Wake up, sleeper!
  Rise from death,
  and Christ will shine on you."

¹⁵So be very careful how you live. Do not live like those who are not wise, but live wisely. ¹⁶Use every chance you have for doing good, because these are evil times. ¹⁷So do not be foolish but learn what the Lord wants you to do. ¹⁸Do not be drunk with wine, which will ruin you, but be filled with the Spirit. ¹⁹Speak to each other with psalms, hymns, and spiritual songs, singing and making music in your hearts to the Lord. ²⁰Always give thanks to God the Father for everything, in the name of our Lord Jesus Christ.

has any inheritance in the kingdom of Christ and God. ⁶Let no one deceive you with empty words, for because of these things the wrath of God comes upon the sons of disobedience. ⁷Therefore do not be partakers with them.

⁸For you were once darkness, but now *you are* light in the Lord. Walk as children of light ⁹(for the fruit of the Spirit *is* in all goodness, righteousness, and truth), ¹⁰finding out what is acceptable to the Lord. ¹¹And have no fellowship with the unfruitful works of darkness, but rather expose *them*. ¹²For it is shameful even to speak of those things which are done by them in secret. ¹³But all things that are exposed are made manifest by the light, for whatever makes manifest is light. ¹⁴Therefore He says:

" Awake, you who sleep,
  Arise from the dead,
  And Christ will give you light."

¹⁵See then that you walk circumspectly, not as fools but as wise, ¹⁶redeeming the time, because the days are evil.

¹⁷Therefore do not be unwise, but understand what the will of the Lord *is*. ¹⁸And do not be drunk with wine, in which is dissipation; but be filled with the Spirit, ¹⁹speaking to one another in psalms and hymns and spiritual songs, singing and making melody in your heart to the Lord, ²⁰giving thanks always for all things to God the Father in the name of our Lord Jesus Christ,

DISCOVERY

Explore the Bible reading by discussing these questions.

2. What kinds of elements would make a joke evil?

_____

_____

_____

3. Describe a life that is full of darkness and a life that is full of light.

_____

_____

_____

4. This passage instructs us to try to learn what pleases God. In what ways can we do that?

_____

_____

_____

5. Why is it shameful even to talk about the evil others do in secret?

_____

_____

_____

6. We probably all know some signs of being drunk with wine. What are some signs of being filled with the Spirit?

_____

_____

_____

INSPIRATION

Here is an uplifting thought from *The Inspirational Bible*.

Almost every headline, every television news report, and every radio bulletin these days proclaims one essential truth: The modern world is in chaos, and no one has a realistic solution. . . .

The whole world is crying out for some word of hope, but all we hear is the babble of wishful thinkers and charlatans. Psychologists, educators, social scientists, physicians, and media wizards of every stripe offer pronouncements and preachments, but even the best ideas generally collapse under closer scrutiny. So far, our modern secular society has produced no positive answers; yet we continue to reach out in hope.

Actually, there is still good reason to hope; there is still time. For with society's failure comes the chance to repent and seek renewal. If we recognize the failures of living without God and turn from our foolishness and disobedience, we may yet be able to receive God's mercy and forgiveness.

Today's headlines are God's warning to a sinful world. The television news flashes are a shadow of His loving hand at work, pushing for the world's redemption. The radio bulletins are a reminder that in spite of our compulsive determination to ruin the earth and destroy God's program of salvation, He has not given up on us completely. Until that day when God's final judgment affixes each of us into place for eternity, there is a chance to begin again. Jesus said, "You must be born again" (John 3:7). That is the last best hope for this world. Ultimately it is our only hope.

(From *Storm Warning* by Billy Graham)

RESPONSE

Use these questions to share more deeply with each other.

7.   Describe the message of hope in the gospel of Jesus Christ.

_____

_____

_____

8.   What words describe a life lived apart from God?

_____

_____

_____

9.   What keeps us from beginning again, when we have every opportunity through God's grace?

_____

_____

_____

PRAYER

God, you've given us such a great promise, the promise of salvation. Forgive us, Father, when we sometimes put more hope in the things of this earth than in the incredible promises of your heaven. Teach us to live in your light.

JOURNALING

Take a few moments to record your personal insights from this lesson.

Why do I sometimes choose darkness instead of light?

ADDITIONAL QUESTIONS

10. Explain how greed becomes idolatry.

_____

_____

_____

11. How can we become more wise?

_____

_____

_____

12. What are the benefits of having hearts filled with gratitude?

_____

_____

_____

For more Bible passages on living in the light, see John 3:19–21; Acts 26:15–18; Romans 13:11–14; 2 Corinthians 4:6; 1 Peter 2:9–10.

To complete the Book of Ephesians during this twelve-part study, read Ephesians 5:1–20.

ADDITIONAL THOUGHTS

LESSON TEN

DON'T MISS THE YIELD SIGNS

REFLECTION

Begin your study by sharing thoughts on this question.

1. Describe a time when you wanted to be mad, but somehow laughter broke through instead.

_____

_____

_____

BIBLE READING

Read Ephesians 5:21–33 from the NCV or the NKJV.

NCV

²¹Yield to obey each other because you respect Christ.

²²Wives, yield to your husbands, as you do to the Lord, ²³because the husband is the head of the wife, as Christ is the head of the church. And he is the Savior of the body, which is the church. ²⁴As the church yields to Christ, so you wives should yield to your husbands in everything.

²⁵Husbands, love your wives as Christ loved the church and gave himself for it ²⁶to make it

NKJV

²¹submitting to one another in the fear of God.

²²Wives, submit to your own husbands, as to the Lord. ²³For the husband is head of the wife, as also Christ is head of the church; and He is the Savior of the body. ²⁴Therefore, just as the church is subject to Christ, so _let_ the wives _be_ to their own husbands in everything.

²⁵Husbands, love your wives, just as Christ also loved the church and gave Himself for her, ²⁶that He might sanctify and cleanse her with

NCV

belong to God. Christ used the word to make the church clean by washing it with water. ²⁷He died so that he could give the church to himself like a bride in all her beauty. He died so that the church could be pure and without fault, with no evil or sin or any other wrong thing in it. ²⁸In the same way, husbands should love their wives as they love their own bodies. The man who loves his wife loves himself. ²⁹No one ever hates his own body, but feeds and takes care of it. And that is what Christ does for the church, ³⁰because we are parts of his body. ³¹The Scripture says, "So a man will leave his father and mother and be united with his wife, and the two will become one body." ³²That secret is very important—I am talking about Christ and the church. ³³But each one of you must love his wife as he loves himself, and a wife must respect her husband.

NKJV

the washing of water by the word, ²⁷that He might present her to Himself a glorious church, not having spot or wrinkle or any such thing, but that she should be holy and without blemish. ²⁸So husbands ought to love their own wives as their own bodies; he who loves his wife loves himself. ²⁹For no one ever hated his own flesh, but nourishes and cherishes it, just as the Lord *does* the church. ³⁰For we are members of His body, of His flesh and of His bones. ³¹"For this reason a man shall leave his father and mother and be joined to his wife, and the two shall become one flesh." ³²This is a great mystery, but I speak concerning Christ and the church. ³³Nevertheless let each one of you in particular so love his own wife as himself, and let the wife *see* that she respects *her* husband.

DISCOVERY

Explore the Bible reading by discussing these questions.

2. What makes it difficult to yield to someone else's wants and needs instead of your own?

_____

_____

_____

3. This passage compares the husband's role in a marriage to Christ's role as the head of the church. What responsibilities then does the husband have?

_____

_____

_____

4. How can wives honor their husbands as the church honors Christ?

_____

_____

_____

5. In what ways can husbands give their lives for their wives as this passage says they should?

_____

_____

_____

6. What is the relationship between love and respect in a marriage?

_____

_____

_____

INSPIRATION

Here is an uplifting thought from *The Inspirational Bible*.

You came home cranky because a deadline got moved up. She came home grumpy because the day-care forgot to give your five-year-old her throat medicine. Each of you was wanting a little sympathy from the other, but neither got any. So there you sit at the dinner table—cranky and grumpy—with little Emily. Emily folds her hands to pray (as she has been taught), and the two of you bow your heads (but not your hearts) and listen. From where this prayer comes, God only knows.

"God, it's Emily. How are you? I'm fine, thank you. Mom and Dad are mad. I don't know why. We've got birds and toys and mashed potatoes and each other. Maybe you can get them to stop being mad? Please do, or it's just gonna be you and me having any fun tonight. Amen."

The prayer is answered before it's finished, you both look up in the middle and laugh at the end and shake your heads and say you're sorry. And you both thank God for the little voice who reminded you about what matters.

That's what "lovebursts" do . . . Lovebursts. Spontaneous affection. Tender moments of radiant love. Ignited devotion. Explosions of tenderness . . . They remind you about what matters. A telegram delivered to the back door of the familiar, telling you to treasure the treasure you've got while you've got it. A whisper from an angel, or someone who sounds like one, reminding you that what you have is greater than what you want and that what is urgent is not always what matters.

(From *He Still Moves Stones*
by Max Lucado)

RESPONSE

Use these questions to share more deeply with each other.

7. When both the husband and wife need the other's sympathy or attention at the same time, how do both get their needs met?

_____

_____

_____

8. List some tactics that help a couple regain perspective when circumstances get tense.

_____

_____

_____

9. Name some issues or circumstances that seem urgent but don't really matter in the long run.

_____

_____

_____

PRAYER

God, give us strength as we try to be more like Jesus in our homes. Keep the evil one away from us. Keep us close to you. Let our homes be testimonies of your love for us. When people look inside, let them see how you have loved the world.

JOURNALING

Take a few moments to record your personal insights from this lesson.

In what ways can I bend more this week to mend a relationship rather than get my own way?

ADDITIONAL QUESTIONS

10. What does it mean to "yield" to someone or something?

_____

_____

_____

11. In what ways is the church like a bride?

_____

_____

_____

12. In what ways will respecting Christ help couples yield to each other?

_____

_____

_____

For more Bible passages on loving marriages, see Colossians 3:18–19; Hebrews 13:4; 1 Peter 3:1–7; .

To complete the Book of Ephesians during this twelve-part study, read Ephesians 5:21–33.

ADDITIONAL THOUGHTS

LESSON ELEVEN

BEING GOOD PARENTS, BEING GOOD BOSSES

REFLECTION

Begin your study by sharing thoughts on this question.

1. What is one of your strongest memories of your mom and/or dad?

_____

_____

_____

BIBLE READING

Read Ephesians 6:1–9 from the NCV or the NKJV.

NCV

¹Children, obey your parents as the Lord wants, because this is the right thing to do. ²The command says, "Honor your father and mother." This is the first command that has a promise with it—³"Then everything will be well with you, and you will have a long life on the earth."

⁴Fathers, do not make your children angry, but raise them with the training and teaching of the Lord.

⁵Slaves, obey your masters here on earth with fear and respect and from a sincere heart,

NKJV

¹Children, obey your parents in the Lord, for this is right. ²"Honor your father and mother," which is the first commandment with promise: ³"that it may be well with you and you may live long on the earth."

⁴And you, fathers, do not provoke your children to wrath, but bring them up in the training and admonition of the Lord.

⁵Bondservants, be obedient to those who are your masters according to the flesh, with fear and trembling, in sincerity of heart, as to Christ;⁶not with eyeservice, as men-pleasers,

NCV

just as you obey Christ. ⁶You must do this not only while they are watching you, to please them. With all your heart you must do what God wants as people who are obeying Christ. ⁷Do your work with enthusiasm. Work as if you were serving the Lord, not as if you were serving only men and women. ⁸Remember that the Lord will give a reward to everyone, slave or free, for doing good.

⁹Masters, in the same way, be good to your slaves. Do not threaten them. Remember that the One who is your Master and their Master is in heaven, and he treats everyone alike.

NKJV

but as bondservants of Christ, doing the will of God from the heart, ⁷with goodwill doing service, as to the Lord, and not to men, ⁸knowing that whatever good anyone does, he will receive the same from the Lord, whether *he is* a slave or free.

⁹And you, masters, do the same things to them, giving up threatening, knowing that your own Master also is in heaven, and there is no partiality with Him.

DISCOVERY

Explore the Bible reading by discussing these questions.

2. God's standard for children is that they obey their parents as God wants them to. Describe that kind of obedience.

3. How can dads keep from making their children angry?

_____

_____

_____

4. In what ways do Paul's instructions to slaves (to work with integrity whether the master is watching or not) apply to employees?

_____

_____

_____

5. Paul reminds masters that they and their slaves are both serving the same master (God). In what ways does this truth apply to bosses or managers?

_____

_____

_____

6. Why would the Bible command us to do our work with enthusiasm?

_____

_____

_____

INSPIRATION

Here is an uplifting thought from *The Inspirational Bible.*

What does it mean to honor your parents? We can see that if we will look at the word *honor* in the Scriptures. In Hebrew, the word for "honor" is *kabed*. This word literally means, "to be heavy, weighty, to honor." Even today, we still link the idea of being heavy with honoring a person.

When the President of the United States or some other important person speaks, people often say that his words "carry a lot of weight." Someone whose words are weighty is someone worthy of honor and respect. However, we can learn even more about what it means to honor someone by looking at its opposite in Scriptures.

. . . The literal meaning of the word "curse" *(qalal)* was "to make light, of little weight, to dishonor." If we go back to our example above, if we dishonor a person we would say, "Their words carry little weight." The contrast is striking!

When Paul tells us to honor our parents, he is telling us that they are worthy of high value and respect. In modern-day terms, we could call them a heavyweight in our lives! Just the opposite is true if we choose to dishonor our parents.

Some people treat their parents as if they are a layer of dust on a table. Dust weighs almost nothing and can be swept away with a brush of the hand. Dust is a nuisance and an eyesore that clouds any real beauty the table might have. Paul tells us that such an attitude should not be a part of how any child views his or her parents and for good reason. If we fail to honor our parents, we not only do what is wrong and dishonor God, but we also literally drain ourselves of life!

(From *The Gift of the Blessing* by Gary Smalley and John Trent)

RESPONSE

Use these questions to share more deeply with each other.

7. In what ways can we honor our parents?

_____

_____

_____

8. What makes honoring our parents difficult?

_____

_____

_____

9. Is disregarding our parents the same as dishonoring them?

_____

_____

_____

PRAYER

Lift up our eyes, Father, that we might see ourselves and those around us as you see us. Help us respond to each other with love and compassion. Help us to be like you.

JOURNALING

Take a few moments to record your personal insights from this lesson.

What can I do to honor my parent(s) or the memory of my parent(s) this week?

ADDITIONAL QUESTIONS

10. In what way is God honored by our diligent work in our jobs?

_____

_____

_____

11. How do you think God will reward everyone for doing good?

_____

_____

_____

12. List some ways employers threaten employees in today's world.

_____

_____

_____

For more Bible passages on parents and children, see Deuteronomy 6:6–9; Proverbs 1:8; 6:20; 22:6; Colossians 3:20; 1 Timothy 3:2–5; Titus 2:3–5.

To complete the Book of Ephesians during this twelve-part study, read Ephesians 6:1–9.

ADDITIONAL THOUGHTS

LESSON TWELVE

BE A WINNER!

REFLECTION

Begin your study by sharing thoughts on this question.

1. Think of a time when you were involved in a big victory of some kind. What are the feelings that come from being on the winning side?

_____

_____

_____

BIBLE READING

Read Ephesians 6:10–20 from the NCV or the NKJV.

NCV

¹⁰Finally, be strong in the Lord and in his great power. ¹¹Put on the full armor of God so that you can fight against the devil's evil tricks. ¹²Our fight is not against people on earth but against the rulers and authorities and the powers of this world's darkness, against the spiritual powers of evil in the heavenly world. ¹³That is why you need to put on God's full armor. Then on the day of evil you will be able to stand strong. And when you have finished the whole fight, you will still be standing. ¹⁴So

NKJV

¹⁰Finally, my brethren, be strong in the Lord and in the power of His might. ¹¹Put on the whole armor of God, that you may be able to stand against the wiles of the devil. ¹²For we do not wrestle against flesh and blood, but against principalities, against powers, against the rulers of the darkness of this age, against spiritual *hosts* of wickedness in the heavenly *places*. ¹³Therefore take up the whole armor of God, that you may be able to withstand in the evil day, and having done all, to stand.

NCV

stand strong, with the belt of truth tied around your waist and the protection of right living on your chest. [15]On your feet wear the Good News of peace to help you stand strong. [16]And also use the shield of faith with which you can stop all the burning arrows of the Evil One. [17]Accept God's salvation as your helmet, and take the sword of the Spirit, which is the word of God. [18]Pray in the Spirit at all times with all kinds of prayers, asking for everything you need. To do this you must always be ready and never give up. Always pray for all God's people.

[19]Also pray for me that when I speak, God will give me words so that I can tell the secret of the Good News without fear. [20]I have been sent to preach this Good News, and I am doing that now, here in prison. Pray that when I preach the Good News I will speak without fear, as I should.

NKJV

[14]Stand therefore, having girded your waist with truth, having put on the breastplate of righteousness, [15]and having shod your feet with the preparation of the gospel of peace; [16]above all, taking the shield of faith with which you will be able to quench all the fiery darts of the wicked one. [17]And take the helmet of salvation, and the sword of the Spirit, which is the word of God; [18]praying always with all prayer and supplication in the Spirit, being watchful to this end with all perseverance and supplication for all the saints—[19]and for me, that utterance may be given to me, that I may open my mouth boldly to make known the mystery of the gospel, [20]for which I am an ambassador in chains; that in it I may speak boldly, as I ought to speak.

DISCOVERY

Explore the Bible reading by discussing these questions.

2. What is the purpose of a soldier's armor?

_____

_____

_____

3. Lists some tricks of the devil this passage might be referring to.

_____

_____

_____

4. In what ways does "right living" protect us?

_____

_____

_____

5. Why do you think the gospel was compared to footwear?

_____

_____

_____

6. List some ways a life of prayer will benefit in spiritual warfare.

_____

_____

_____

INSPIRATION

Here is an uplifting thought from *The Inspirational Bible*.

Triumph is a precious thing. We honor the triumphant. The gallant soldier sitting astride his steed. The determined explorer returning from his discovery. The winning athlete holding aloft the triumphant trophy of victory. Yes, we love triumph.

Triumph brings with it a swell of purpose and meaning. When I'm triumphant, I'm worthy. When I'm triumphant, I count. When I'm triumphant, I'm significant.

Triumph is fleeting, though. Hardly does one taste victory before it is gone; achieved, yet now history. No one remains champion forever. Time for yet another conquest, another victory. Perhaps this is the absurdity of Paul's claim: "But thanks be to God, who always leads us in triumphal procession . . ." (2 Cor. 2:14).

The triumph of Christ is not temporary. "Triumphant in Christ" is not an event or an occasion. It's not fleeting. To be triumphant in Christ is a life-style . . . a state of being! To triumph in Christ is not something we do, it's something we are.

Here is the big difference between victory in Christ and victory in the world: A victor in the world rejoices over something he did—swimming the English Channel, climbing Mt. Everest, making a million. But the believer rejoices over who he is: a child of God, a forgiven sinner, an heir of eternity. As the hymn goes, "heir of salvation, purchase of God, born of his Spirit, washed in his blood."

Nothing can separate us from our triumph in Christ. Nothing! Our triumph is not based upon our feelings but upon God's gift. Our triumph is based not upon our perfection but upon God's forgiveness. How precious is this triumph! For even though we are pressed on every side, the victory is still ours. Nothing can alter the loyalty of God.

A friend of mine recently lost his father to death. The faith of his father had for years served as an inspiration for many. In moments alone with the body of his father, my friend said this thought kept coming to his mind as he looked at his daddy's face: "You won. You won. You won!" As Joan of Arc said when she was abandoned by those who should have stood by her, "It is better to be alone with God. His friendship will not fail me, nor his counsel, nor his love. In his strength I will dare and dare and dare until I die."

"Triumphant in Christ." It is not something we do. It's something we are.

(From *On the Anvil*
by Max Lucado)

RESPONSE

Use these questions to share more deeply with each other.

7. In what ways are Christians like soldiers?

_____

_____

_____

8. Define spiritual victory.

_____

_____

_____

9. How does the armor described in Ephesians equip us for our battles?

_____

_____

_____

PRAYER

We give you praise. We honor and glorify your name. You truly are the King of kings and the Lord of lords. We thank you and worship you and will follow you forever and ever. Amen.

JOURNALING

Take a few moments to record your personal insights from this lesson.

How can I put on the full protective armor of God this week?

ADDITIONAL QUESTIONS

10. In what way is faith like a shield?

_____

_____

_____

11. How is salvation like a helmet?

_____

_____

_____

12. In what way is the Word of God like a sword?

_____

_____

_____

For more Bible passages on victory in Christ, see Psalm 44:4–8; 60:12; 118:13–16; Proverbs 2:6–8; 21:30–31; 1 Corinthians 15:54–57; 1 John 5:3–5.

To complete the Book of Ephesians during this twelve-part study, read Ephesians 6:10–23.

ADDITIONAL THOUGHTS

ADDITIONAL THOUGHTS

ADDITIONAL THOUGHTS

LEADERS' NOTES

LESSON ONE

Question 2: Like Ephesians, the Book of 1 Peter begins with a wonderful tribute to the spiritual blessings we have through Christ. Read 1 Peter 1:3–9 for another expression of praise for all that we have been given in Jesus.

Question 5: For this, and any other question where group members may be deeply divided in their answers, discourage members from simply airing their personal opinions. Instead, encourage them to base their answers on what they find in God's Word.

LESSON TWO

Question 7: This question could lead to an involved discussion. The relationship between God's sovereignty and man's will is one that has been widely debated in the church for centuries. If you want to keep from spending too much time on this issue during your study, encourage group members to stick to what they can learn from the text in Ephesians in answering this question. You could then use any extra time you may have at the end of the study to come back and discuss the issue further.

Question 10: More on God's relationship to his church can be found in Ephesians 5:22–32 and Colossians 1:18–20.

LESSON THREE

Question 2: Keep in mind that the goal of this question is to explore God's mercy and grace by looking at the state we were in when God saved us and all that he rescued us from. It is not a time to brag about past sin.

Question 4: It might help to have the group discuss the characteristics of something that is *physically* dead, and then carry this over into the discussion of what it means to be *spiritually* dead.

Question 6: Lead this discussion into not only *why* but what are the dangers of relating our salvation to our efforts. When we perceive our salvation as coming from anything that we do, we take the credit for something that God alone has accomplished. We unwittingly seek to rob him of the glory that should be only his.

LESSON FOUR

Question 5: You may want to have the group look at Romans 8:13–17. These verses speak of the intimate relationship God has granted to us as his children.

Question 11: Does anyone in your group have any knowledge of architecture? Find out what they know about the purpose of a cornerstone. While the cornerstones on most present-day buildings are primarily decorative, when Ephesians was written they served a much more important purpose. The cornerstone was placed with precision and care, because the rest of the building rested upon it and was aligned with it. Keep this in mind as you answer the question.

LESSON FIVE

Question 2: For a partial list of Paul's sufferings, you can look at 2 Corinthians 11:16–33.

Question 9: A good verse to start with might be 1 John 3:16, where it says, "This is how we know what real love is: Jesus gave his life for us." Other verses you can use as a springboard for discussing this question are John 3:16, Romans 5:6–10, and 1 John 4:9–10.

LESSON SIX

Question 8: For examples of Jesus' compassion, you can look at his responses to the crowds in Matthew 9:36–38, 14:13–14, and 15:29–39, and at his interactions with the two blind men in Matthew 20:29–34, with the leper in Mark 1:40–42, with the grieving mother in Luke 7:11–15, and with Jairus and the hemorrhaging woman in Luke 8:40–56.

Question 9: Keep in mind that this question concerns our perception of God's love, not whether he loves us or not. While the choices we make will affect that perception, there is nothing a believer can do to remove themselves from it. Romans 8:35–39 reminds us that nothing, *absolutely nothing*, in heaven or on earth can separate us from the love of God.

Question 12: You may also want to consider whether there are any ministries that are not a part of the church, but that should be, in order for the church to fully reflect Jesus' care for people.

LESSON SEVEN

Question 3: You can help group members identify ways to accept each other through some of the following questions: Who are the people that you feel most comfortable with? Who are the people that you know will always love and accept you no matter what you might do? How is it that those people have made you feel this way? In what ways have they shown their acceptance of you?

Question 8: If you'd like to further explore what it means to live a spirit-filled life, have the group read and discuss Galatians 5:16–26.

Question 12: In answer to this question, it might help to have the group look at Colossians 3:1–17. In this passage we find an exhortation to humility, gentleness, and patience that comes on the heels of a description of those things that belong to the earthly nature—those things that keep us from following that exhortation.

LESSON EIGHT

Question 6: The Book of Proverbs has a great deal to say about the power of our words and how we should be using them. Challenge group members to read through at least one verse in Proverbs each day. Some that are particularly applicable to this subject are Proverbs 11:13, 12:18–19, 13:3, 15:1–2, 15:4, 16:24, 25:12, 25:15, 28:23, and 31:26.

Question 10: Ephesians 4:22–24 provides us with a formula for growth—in the area of bitterness and anger, as well as others. First, we are told to leave our "old self," and stop doing the things that accompany it, such as bitterness. Then we are told to be made new in our hearts; Romans 12:2 tells us that this happens as we renew our minds. As we fill our minds with the truths of God's Word, our hearts are changed. Next, we are told to become a "new person," and start doing the things that accompany it, such as being kind and loving. Ephesians 4:31–32 gives us specifics; we are not only told what we should stop doing but also what we should start doing instead. It's much easier to stop a sinful habit when we replace it with a godly one!

LESSON NINE

Question 6: When a person is drunk with wine (or some other form of alcohol), their actions are being controlled by that wine. Paul is comparing the control that alcohol can have over the body to the control that the Spirit should have over the believer.

Question 7: The hope that we have in the gospel of Jesus is a prominent theme throughout the New Testament. Some related Scriptures are Galatians 5:5, Colossians 1:3–5, Titus 2:12–14, and 1 John 3:2–3.

Question 11: The Book of Proverbs provides a great source of practical wisdom for daily living. Encourage group members to become familiar with the wonderful nuggets of truth found there. Some passages on wisdom are Proverbs 2:6; 2:12; 3:19; 4:5–7; 9:10; 9:12; 11:2; 12:8; 13:10; 14:8; 14:33; 16:16; 17:24; 18:4; 19:8; 19:11.

LESSON TEN

Question 1: For anyone with kids, this question shouldn't be difficult to answer. Children have an incredible ability to disobey while being cute and funny at the same time! Take some time laughing about each other's stories.

Question 4: If your group contains both males and females, consider having the men answer this question first, before you give the women a chance to answer. (And you may want to require the women to answer before the men in question 5.)

Question 11: In Revelation 21:1–5 you can find a description of the bride of Christ.

LESSON ELEVEN

Question 7: We usually concentrate on what it means for children to honor their parents when the children are still quite young. But it's equally important to consider what this means as we get older. What does it mean to honor your parents as a college student? Or as a newly married couple? How do you honor your parents as they grow old and possibly degenerate mentally and physically?

Question 12: In light of your answers to these questions, you may want to take some time to have group members reflect on changes they need to make in their roles as employees and/or bosses. Encourage each person to think through ways they can grow in their obedience to the instructions given here.

LESSON TWELVE

Question 9: If you have time, take a few moments and ask the group to spend it in quiet reflection on this passage. Encourage them to evaluate just how "battle ready" they are. What changes do they need to make each day to ensure that they are fully equipped for battle? You may then want to share with each other, and take some time to pray for one another in these areas.

Question 12: Challenge your group to become more adept at using their sword. Encourage them to spend time in the Word of God each day, to talk about it with others, to memorize it, and to think about it!

ADDITIONAL NOTES

ADDITIONAL NOTES

ADDITIONAL NOTES

ADDITIONAL NOTES

ADDITIONAL NOTES

ADDITIONAL NOTES

ACKNOWLEDGMENTS

Graham, Billy. *Peace with God*, copyright 1984 Word, Inc., Dallas, Texas.

Graham, Billy. *Storm Warning*, copyright 1992, Word Inc., Dallas, Texas.

Lucado, Max. *God Came Near*, Questar Publishers, Multnomah Books, copyright 1987, by Max Lucado.

Lucado, Max. *He Still Moves Stones*, copyright 1993, Word Inc., Dallas, Texas.

Lucado, Max. *No Wonder They Call Him the Savior*, Questar Publishers, Multnomah Books, copyright 1986 by Max Lucado.

Lucado, Max. *On the Anvil*, copyright 1985 by Max Lucado. Used by permission of Tyndale House Publishers, Inc. All rights reserved.

MacDonald, William, *Alone in Majesty*, copyright 1994 Thomas Nelson, Nashville, Tennessee.

Smalley, Gary and Trent, John. *A Dad's Blessing*, copyright 1994 Thomas Nelson, Nashville, Tennessee.

Smalley, Gary and Trent, John. *The Gift of the Blessing*, copyright 1993 Thomas Nelson, Nashville, Tennessee.

Stanley, Charles. *The Wonderful Spirit-Filled Life*, copyright 1992 Thomas Nelson, Nashville, Tennessee.